North American Indian Portraits

Encampment of Piekann Indians

North American Indian Portraits

120 Full-Color Plates
from
The McKenney-Hall
Portrait Gallery of
American Indians

By James D. Horan

Crown Publishers, Inc. • New York

Published 1975 by Crown Publishers, Inc.

Inquiries should be addressed to
Crown Publishers, Inc., 419 Park Avenue South, New York, N.Y. 10016
Library of Congress Catalog Card Number: 75-15420
ISBN: 0-517-524570

Published simultaneously in Canada by General Publishing
Company Limited
Printed in Italy by A. Mondadori, Verona

The Plates

These portraits were painted from life, almost all during the 1830s, by Charles Bird King, James Otto Lewis, and other outstanding American artists. The period has been called The Golden Age of the American Indian. The originals of these portraits from the McKenney-Hall Portrait Gallery of American Indians, published in 1836, were exhibited for many years at the Smithsonian Institution until they were destroyed by fire in 1865.

1. Joseph Brant, Thayendanegea	*Iroquois*
2. Red Jacket	*Iroquois*
3. Cornplanter, Kiontwogky, or Handsome Lake	*Iroquois*
4. Ahyouwaighs, or John Brant	*Iroquois*
5. McIntosh	*Creek*
6. Apauly Tustennuggee	*Creek*
7. Ledagie	*Creek*
8. Oche Finceco	*Creek*
9. Selocta	*Creek*
10. Menawa, the Great Warrior	*Creek*
11. Tustennuggee Emathla	*Creek*
12. Paddy Carr	*Creek*
13. Yoholo-Micco	*Creek*
14. Mistippee	*Creek*
15. Opothle-Yaholo	*Creek*
16. Waapashaw	*Sioux*
17. Wanata, or the Charger	*Sioux*
18. Little Crow	*Sioux*
19. Eshtahumbah, or Sleepy Eyes	*Sioux*
20. Moukaushka, or the Trembling Earth	*Sioux*
21. Tokacou	*Sioux*
22. Tenskwatawa, the Prophet, Brother of Tecumseh	*Shawnee*
23. Catahecassa, or Black Hoof	*Shawnee*
24. Paytakootha, or Flying Clouds	*Shawnee*
25. Quatawapea, or Colonel Lewis	*Shawnee*
26. Kishkalwa	*Shawnee*
27. War Dance	*Winnebago*
28. Makataimeshekiakiah, or Black Hawk	*Sauk and Fox*
29. Keokuk, Chief of the Sauk and Fox Nation	*Sauk and Fox*
30. Keesheswa	*Sauk and Fox*
31. Keesheewaa	*Sauk and Fox*
32. Wakechai, or Crouching Eagle	*Sauk and Fox*
33. Kaipolequa, or White-nosed Fox	*Sauk and Fox*
34. Powasheek	*Sauk and Fox*
35. Taiomah	*Sauk and Fox*
36. Appanoose	*Sauk and Fox*
37. Wapella, or the Prince	*Sauk and Fox*
38. Kishkekosh	*Sauk and Fox*
39. Nesouaquoit, or the Bear in the Forks of a Tree	*Sauk and Fox*

40. Peahmuska	*Sauk and Fox*
41. Pashepahaw, or the Stabber	*Sauk and Fox*
42. Tahcoloquoit	*Sauk and Fox*
43. Weshcubb, or the Sweet	*Chippewa*
44. Metakoosega, or Pure Tobacco	*Chippewa*
45. Shingaba W'Ossin	*Chippewa*
46. Ohyawamincekee	*Chippewa*
47. Peechekir	*Chippewa*
48. Waatopenot	*Chippewa*
49. Jackopa, or the Six	*Chippewa*
50. Ongewae	*Chippewa*
51. Pashenine	*Chippewa*
52. No-Tin	*Chippewa*
53. Katawabeda	*Chippewa*
54. Wabishkeepenas, or the White Pigeon	*Chippewa*
55. Waemboeshkaa	*Chippewa*
56. Okeemakeequid	*Chippewa*
57. Caatousee	*Chippewa*
58. Anacamegishca, or Foot Prints	*Chippewa*
59. Tshusick	*Chippewa*
60. Chippewa Squaw and Child	*Chippewa*
61. A Chippewa Widow	*Chippewa*
62. Chippewa Mother and Child	*Chippewa*
63. Petalesharo, the Bravest of the Brave	*Pawnee*
64. Peskelechaco	*Pawnee*
65. Sharitarish	*Pawnee*
66. Osceola (Aseola)	*Seminole*
67. Halpatter-Micco, or Billy Bowlegs	*Seminole*
68. Julcee Mathla	*Seminole*
69. Itcho Tustennuggee	*Seminole*
70. Tukosee Mathla	*Seminole*
71. Yahahajo	*Seminole*
72. Micanopy	*Seminole*
73. Foke Luste Hajo	*Seminole*
74. Neamathla	*Seminole*
75. Chittee-Yoholo	*Seminole*
76. Sequoyah, or George Guess	*Cherokee*
77. Major Ridge	*Cherokee*
78. John Ridge	*Cherokee*
79. Tahchee, or Dutch	*Cherokee*
80. John Ross	*Cherokee*
81. David Vann	*Cherokee*
82. Tooan Tuh, or Spring Frog	*Cherokee*
83. Red Bird	*Winnebago*
84. Nawkaw, or Wood	*Winnebago*
85. Tshizunhaukau	*Winnebago*
86. Wakawn, or the Snake	*Winnebago*
87. Wakaunhaka, or the Snake Skin	*Winnebago*
88. Amisquam, or Wooden Ladle	*Winnebago*
89. Hoowanneka, or Little Elk	*Winnebago*
90. A Winnebago Orator	*Winnebago*

Joseph Brant

Red Jacket

Cornplanter

Ahyouwaighs

McIntosh

Apauly Tustennuggee

Ledagie

Oche Finceco

Selocta

Menawa

Tustennuggee Emathla

Paddy Carr

Yoholo-Micco

Mistippee

Opothle-Yaholo

Waapashaw

Wanata

Little Crow

Eshtahumbah

Moukaushka

Tokacou

Tenskwatawa

Catahecassa

Paytakootha

Quatawapea

Kishkalwa

War Dance

Makataimeshekiakiah

Keokuk

Keesheswa

Keesheewaa

Wakechai

Kaipolequa

Powasheek

Taiomah

Appanoose

Wapella

Kishkekosh

Nesouaquoit

Peahmuska

Pashepahaw

Tahcoloquoit

Weshcubb

Metakoosega

Shingaba W'Ossin

Ohyawamincekee

Peechekir

Waatopenot

Jackopa

Ongewae

Pashenine

No-Tin

Katawabeda

Wabishkeepenas

Waemboeshkaa

Okeemakeequid

Caatousee

Anacamegishca

Tshusick

Chippewa Squaw and Child

A Chippewa Widow

Chippewa Mother and Child

Petalesharo

Peskelechaco

Sharitarish

Osceola

Billy Bowlegs

Julcee Mathla

Itcho Tustennuggee

Tukosee Mathla

Yahahajo

Micanopy

Foke Luste Hajo

Neamathla

Chittee-Yoholo

Sequoyah

Major Ridge

John Ridge

Tahchee

John Ross

David Vann

Tooan Tuh

Red Bird

Nawkaw

Tshizunhaukau

Wakawn

Wakaunhaka

Amisquam

Hoowanneka

A Winnebago Orator

L'Ietan

Hayne Hudjihini

Choncape

Nowaykesugga

Mahaskah

Rantchewaime

Mahaskah the Younger

Shauhaunapotinia

Moanahonga

Notchimine

Neomonni

Tahrohon

Watchemonne

Tishcohan

Lappawinze

Pocahontas

Metea

Wabaunsee

Shahaka

Pushmataha

Mohongo

Le Soldat du Chene

Stumanu

Monchonsia

Kanapima

Timpoochee Barnard

Nahetluchopie

Ongpatonga

Amiskquew

Markomete